Mommy, Where's My Daddy?

For Children Who Have Lost a Parent

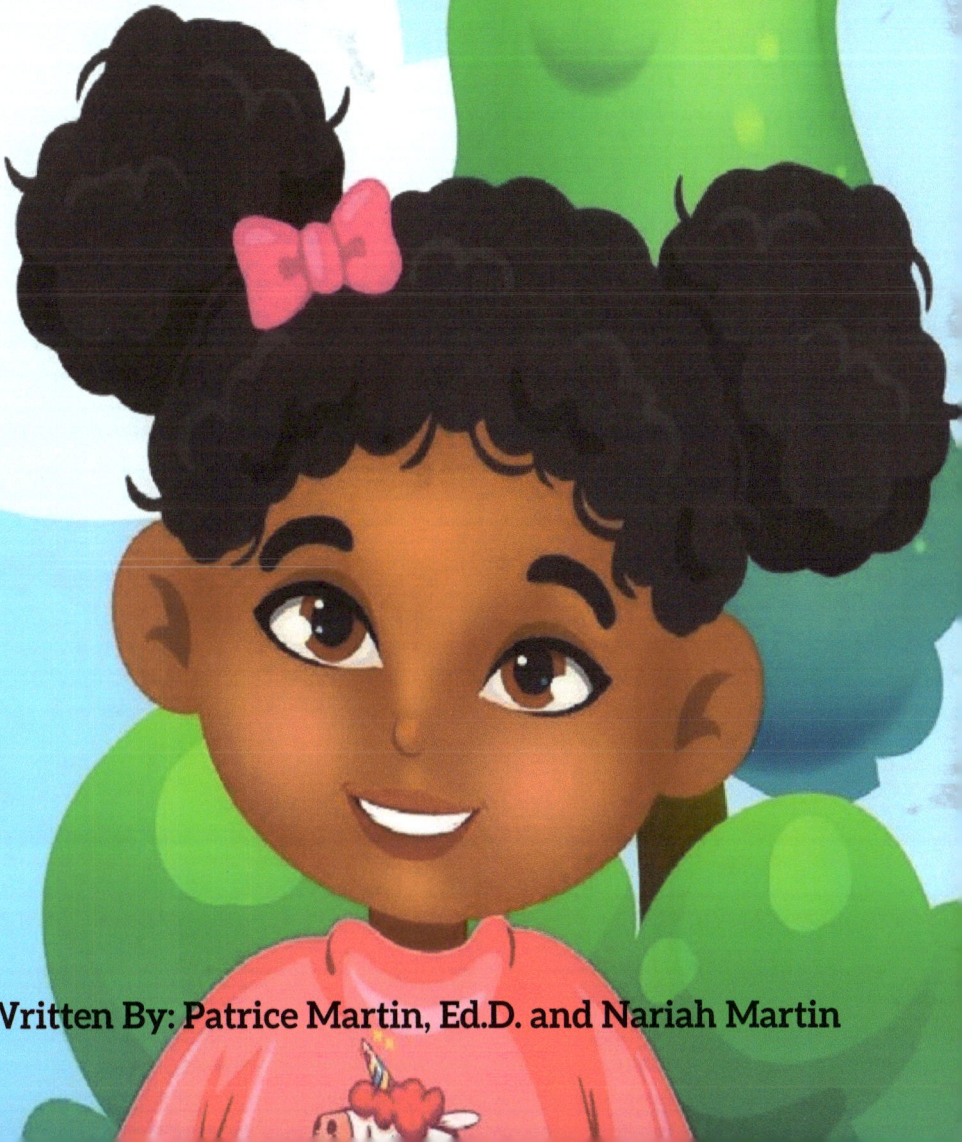

Written By: Patrice Martin, Ed.D. and Nariah Martin

Mommy, Where's My Daddy? For Children Who Have Lost a Parent
Written By: Patrice Martin, Ed.D. and Nariah Martin

Scripture Public Domain NKJV

Illustrated By: Rida Zubairi

Self Publishing Services: Kimberly Ivory Taylor / PURSUE KIM LLC

ISBN : 979-8-218-31674-7

PURSUE K.I.M

Mommy, Where's My Daddy?
For Children Who Have Lost a Parent

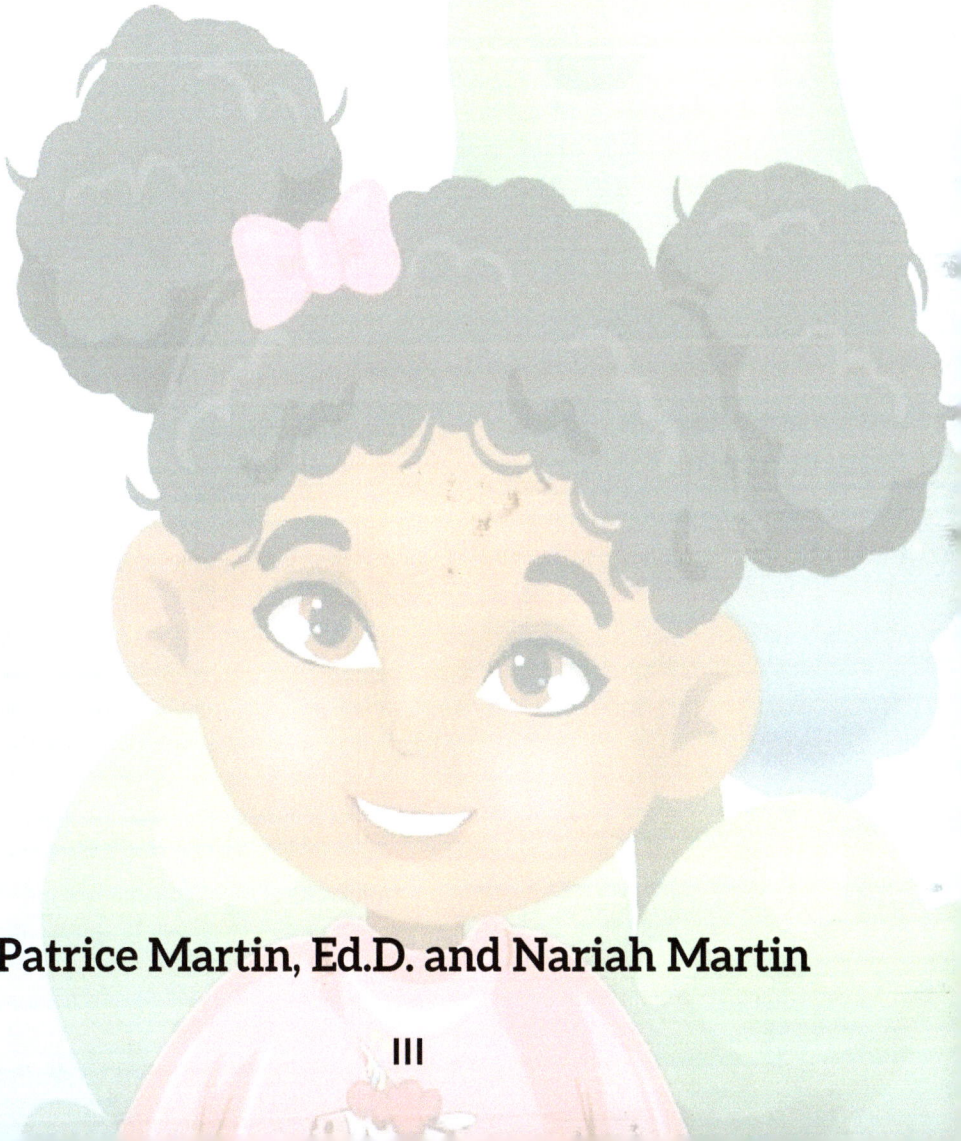

Patrice Martin, Ed.D. and Nariah Martin

Acknowledgments

I would like to acknowledge my Lord and Savior Jesus Christ. Without Him, this book would not be possible.

It would have been impossible to complete this process without the support from my Mom and Dad, my sisters, and my children.

I'd also like to acknowledge my publisher's support throughout this process has been invaluable.

Dedication Page

To children whose parents lost their lives due to illness, violence, and unforeseen circumstances. May their memories live on through you and give you comfort!

To my deceased husband, Wallace: You were a wonderful husband, a great father, and our biggest cheerleader. Although you are not here physically, your spirit continues to live on.

To my daughter, Nariah: Thank you for opening your heart to the world and being brave enough to ask the hard question. "Mommy, Where's My Daddy?"

Purpose

The purpose of writing this children's book titled "Mommy, Where's My Daddy?" For Children Who Have Lost a Parent is to provide comfort, support, and guidance to young readers facing this challenging and emotional situation. The book aims to support children in their grief journey, helping them find comfort and understanding during a difficult and emotional time in their lives.

John 14: 1-3 NKJV

14 "Let not your heart be troubled; you believe in God, believe also in Me. 2 In My Father's house are many [a]mansions; if it were not so, [b]I would have told you. I go to prepare a place for you. 3 And if I go and prepare a place for you, I will come again and receive you to Myself; that where I am, there you may be also.

Introduction

You see, Nariah's dad died of leukemia when she was only 2 years old. At 4 years old, she starts to notice that her father is not present in her life, and she has become curious. She notices that other children have their father in their lives, and she does not. Although Nariah's father was very active in the early stages of her life, she recognizes he's now no longer present. It's now time to have the conversation. This story is an actual conversation between Nariah and her mother.

One day Nariah's mother was in the kitchen washing dishes.

Nariah walks into the kitchen and asks, "Mommy, Where's My Daddy?"

So Nariah's mother turns and says, "Do you remember what we talked about?"

10

Nariah's mother explained to her
that her dad had been sick in the
hospital and then went to heaven.
She just needed a reminder.

"Your daddy is in heaven," said mom.

Nariah asks, "What's heaven?"

"It's a beautiful place in the sky where God lives," said mom.

"Is he coming back?"
asked Nariah.

Nariah's mother says, "No, he's not coming back, but we can always look at his pictures. Would you like to turn on the memory lamp?" asks mom.

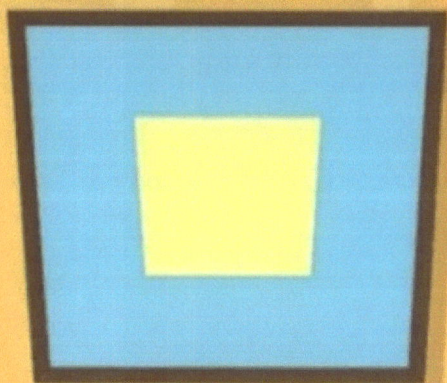

"Ok," Nariah says.
And together, Nariah and
her mom turn on the
memory lamp.

We use the
memory lamp
to remember
those we love
who are no
longer with
us.

Because
Someone we love
is in Heaven
there's a little bit of
Heaven

PASTE A
PICTURE OF
YOUR LOVE
ONE IN
HEAVEN

Writing Activity

Instructions: Ask your child to think about the person they want to write about (parent or loved one who has passed away). Use prompt and the lines below to write how they feel.

Writing Prompt: How did you feel when your parent or loved one went to heaven?

_____

_____

_____

_____

_____

_____

_____

_____

_____

Memory Book Activity

A simple and age-appropriate student activity to help a child cope with the death of a parent or loved one is to create a "Memory Book." This activity allows a child to remember and celebrate the positive memories they shared with their parent.

Materials Needed:

1. Blank notebook or a few sheets of paper
2. Crayons, markers, or colored pencils
3. Family photos or pictures of the deceased parent (optional)
4. Glue (if using photos)
5. Stickers or decorative materials (optional)

Steps:

1. Introduction: Start by explaining that you are going to make a special book together that will help the child remember and cherish the happy times they had with their parent.

2. Decorate the Cover: Let the child decorate the cover of the notebook or paper using crayons, markers, stickers, or any decorative materials you have. You can also include a picture of the parent who passed away if appropriate.

3. Create Memory Pages: Help the child create pages for the Memory Book. Each page can represent a different memory or something they loved about their parent. For example:

- "When we went to the park together"
- "My favorite bedtime story"
- "A special meal we shared"

4. Add Pictures: If you have family photos or pictures of the parent, you can glue these onto the corresponding pages. Encourage the child to talk about each photo and the memory associated with it.

5. Draw Pictures: If you don't have photos, the child can draw pictures on each page to represent their memories. For example, they can draw a picture of themselves playing at the park.

6. Describe the Memories: Ask the child to describe each memory in their own words. Write down what they say on the pages, even if it's just a few simple words or sentences. This helps the child express their feelings and thoughts.

7. Decorate Each Page: Encourage the child to decorate each page with drawings, colors, or stickers to make it special.

8. Read the Memory Book: Once the Memory Book is complete, read it together with the child. Talk about the memories, ask questions, and allow the child to share their feelings and thoughts.

9. Keep the Memory Book Safe: Explain that this book is a safe place to keep their special memories, and they can look at it whenever they miss their parent or want to remember the good times.

10. Add New Memories: Over time, encourage the child to add new memories to the book as they create them. This can be an ongoing activity that helps them continue to cope with their loss.

The Memory Book provides a tangible and creative way for the child to remember their parent and express their emotions. It can also serve as a valuable keepsake in the years to come.

Purpose

The purpose of writing this children's book titled "Mommy, Where's My Daddy?" For Children Who Have Lost a Parent is to provide comfort, support, and guidance to young readers facing this challenging and emotional situation. The book aims to:

1. Offer Emotional Support: Help children cope with their grief and feelings of loss by addressing their emotions and reassuring them that it's okay to feel sad or confused.

2. Provide a Safe Space for Expression: Create a safe and relatable story that allows children to express their feelings, ask questions, and begin to process their emotions.

3. Normalize Grief: Show that grieving is a natural part of life and that they are not alone in their experiences. By featuring characters who have gone through similar situations, the book can help children feel understood and less isolated.

4. Explain the Concept of Loss: Use age-appropriate language and storytelling techniques to help children understand the concept of death and loss in a gentle and sensitive manner.

5. Encourage Communication: Promote open communication between children and their caregivers, encouraging them to share their thoughts and concerns.

6. Offer Coping Strategies: Provide simple coping strategies and tools that can help children navigate their grief, such as creating memory keepsakes or talking to a trusted adult.

7. Celebrate Positive Memories: Highlight the importance of cherishing positive memories of the parent who has passed away, fostering a sense of connection and love.

8. Foster Resilience: Help children develop resilience and emotional strength as they navigate the grieving process, ultimately moving toward healing and acceptance. In essence, the purpose of "Mommy, Where's My Daddy?" is to support children in their grief journey, helping them find comfort and understanding during a difficult and emotional time in their lives

10 Tips for Family Members

Helping a child grieve the loss of a parent can be a challenging and delicate process. Here are some tips to provide support and comfort during this difficult time:

1. Use simple and age-appropriate language: Explain the situation in a clear and gentle manner, using words and concepts that a child can understand. Avoid euphemisms like "passed away" or "gone to sleep" as they can be confusing.

2. Maintain routines: Children find comfort in routines and familiarity. Try to maintain their daily routines as much as possible to provide stability and security.

3. Encourage expression: Allow your child to express their feelings and thoughts in their own way. They may not have the words to describe their emotions, so be patient and open to different forms of expression like drawing, playing, or storytelling.

4. Be available: Make yourself available for your child to talk or ask questions about the deceased parent. Answer their questions honestly and be prepared to repeat information as needed, as young children may not fully understand or remember the details of the situation.

5. Offer reassurance: Reassure your child that you are there for them and that you will take care of them. Let them know that it's okay to feel sad, angry, or confused and that these feelings are normal.

6. Provide comfort objects: Some children may find comfort in a special toy, blanket, or other objects that remind them of the deceased parent. Encourage the use of these comfort objects when needed.

7. Read books about grief: There are many children's books available that address the topic of grief and loss. Reading such books together can help your child understand their feelings and the grieving process.

8. Seek professional help: If you notice signs of prolonged or intense distress, consider consulting with a child psychologist or counselor who specializes in grief and loss. They can provide strategies and support tailored to your child's specific needs.

9. Connect with support networks: Join a local support group for grieving families or seek out online communities where you can connect with others who have experienced similar losses. Sharing experiences and advice with others can be comforting.

10. Take care of yourself: Remember that you also need support during this difficult time.

Seek help from friends, family, or a therapist to cope with your own grief and to ensure that you can continue to provide emotional support to your child. Remember that every child is unique, and their grieving process will unfold differently. It's essential to be patient, flexible, and attuned to your child's needs as they navigate their grief journey.

Summary

As a result of this lost, Patrice gives Nariah the freedom and space to ask questions about her dad and also to discuss death and all it entails. Although these discussions are challenging, Nariah continues to grow in her understanding of death and the importance of exploring life.

Meet the Authors

Dr. Patrice Martin is an author, educator, Pastor, entrepreneur, and the mother of one daughter, Nariah and two sons Corbrierre and Brent. Patrice has worked in the field of education for over 25 years. She has served in the field of education at the local, state, and federal level. Her expertise involves supporting districts and schools with the greatest needs, leading teams, providing effective coaching and feedback, and building leadership capacity for the purpose of improving student outcomes and close academic gaps. Patrice enjoys spending time with family, traveling, and music.

Nariah Martin is an author and she's currently a 2nd grade student. She enjoys playing with her dolls, watching shows on her iPad, and Burger King fries. Patrice and Nariah reside in Jackson, Tennessee.

Meet the Illustrator

Rida Zubairi is an illustrator offering years of experience in design. She has worked in gaming studio along with other various companies. Recently, she has worked with Dtale Communication as an Art Director, MCIT gaming studio as a Senior CG Artist, and Team Lead at Expert Solution. Rida currently resides in Pakistan.

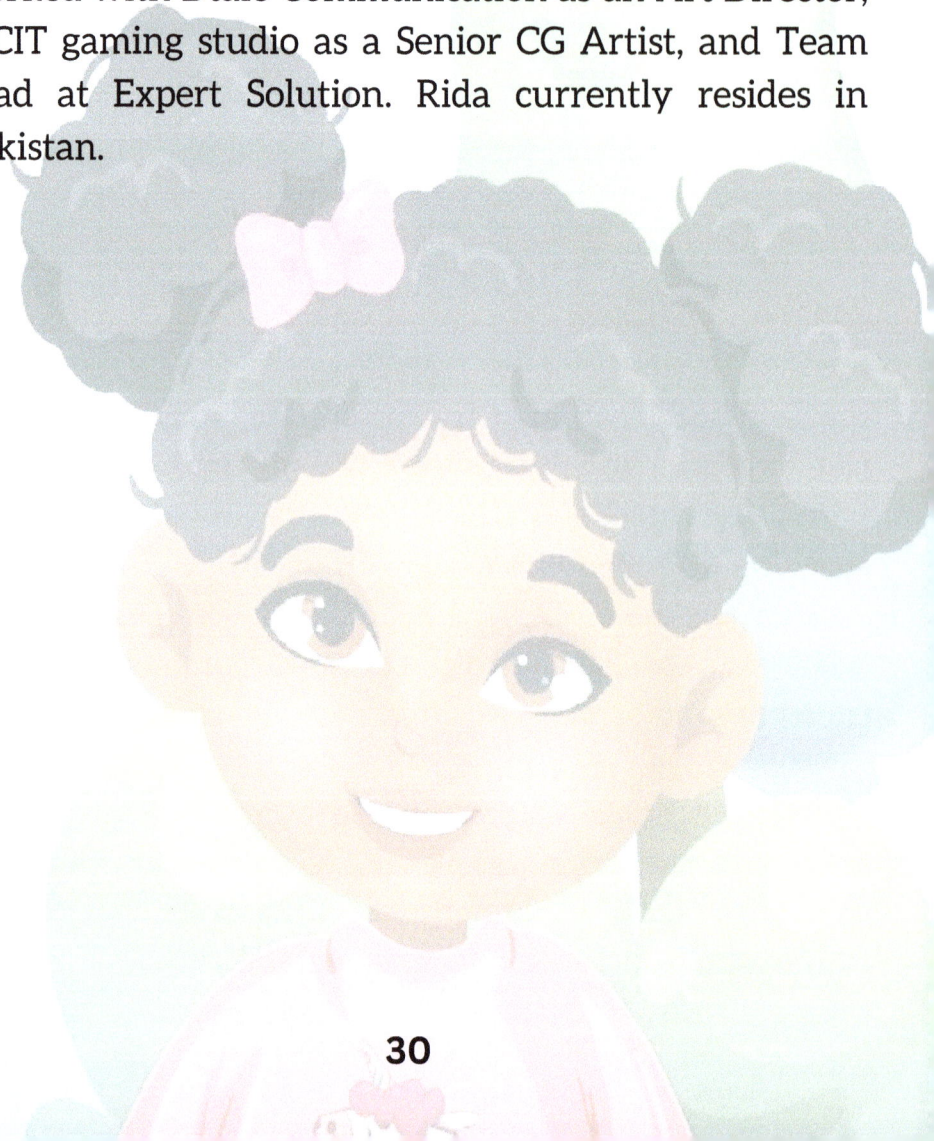

Stay Connected

Email

Mommywheresmydaddy@gmail.com

Website

www.mommywheresmydaddy.com

www.ingramcontent.com/pod-product-compliance
Lightning Source LLC
Chambersburg PA
CBHW040035110426
42741CB00030B/30